The Towers & Steeples Designed By Sir Christopher Wren

Si·Monumentum·requiris·circumspice·

The Towers & Steeples

Designed by

Sir Christopher Wren

RESVRGAM

A descriptive historical & critical Essay. with Numerous Illustrations.

by Andrew T. Taylor ARIBA Architect

London
B.T. Batsford High Holborn.
1881.

PREFACE.

———

THE substance of the following pages was originally written in the form of an Essay, which recently gained the Medal of the Royal Institute of British Architects. Having thus met with some acceptance, and the subject being one of great interest,—especially at the present time, when it has disturbed even the calm atmosphere of the House of Lords, the Author has ventured to publish it, after careful revision, and with the addition of several illustrations.

The Plans and Sections of some of Sir Christopher Wren's most important examples may be found useful to those professionally engaged, who have not hitherto had an opportunity of studying their construction; and the complete series of Sketches may be interesting to the public generally, as evidencing the versatility of Wren's genius.

The Sketches of the existing Towers and Steeples in London have, in every instance, been made by the Author on the spot, and, however imperfect they may be in draughtsmanship, it is hoped they may at

a

least be found to have some value as authentic records;
while, for those which have been pulled down, no pains
have been spared in obtaining, from the most reliable
sources, accurate information and correct representations
of them, and from these the Sketches have been made.
In the production of the Scale Plans and Sections,
indebtedness is heartily acknowledged to Mr. Clayton's
excellent drawings, for valuable help.

The Author is happy also to take this opportunity
of expressing his obligations to those who have assisted
him in verifying facts and obtaining information relative
to the special Churches with which they were con-
nected; and especially to the Rev. H. Cummins, the
Rev. W. Denton, the Rev. J. Jackson, the Rev. W.
Sparrow Simpson, D.D., the Rev. A. Trower, the Rev.
M. Vine, Major Joseph, and H. Wright, Esq.

A. T. T.

MOORGATE CHAMBERS,
72, FINSBURY PAVEMENT, E.C.

CONTENTS.

vi.

LIST OF ILLUSTRATIONS.

THE

TOWERS & STEEPLES

Designed by

➤✳ Sir Christopher Wren. ✳◄

🌿

NATURE abhors uniformity: there is infinite variety in all her phases. The sea, now calm, reflecting the beauty of cloudland, and anon surging and leaping with great crested waves in irresistible power; the sky, now wrapt in mantle of purest blue, now lit up with golden glory, and anon black with mountains of piled-up vapours; the landscape, with hill and valley, rock and tree, ever varying and changing as the lights and shadows pass—all demonstrate this fact. A flat, level expanse of country is not beautiful in itself, although it may be useful—it is the prose of Nature: the poetry and majesty and power is in her uplands, her deep dells, her hills and her mountains.

It is almost a trite saying, that if we would not err, we must study the laws and the principles of Nature; yet it is one which cannot be too often reiterated and kept in remembrance. Our Cities are the outcome of our needs and pursuits; and we shall best consult their fitness and beauty, by applying to them those elements which Nature displays in her realm.

Imagine, if possible, a city composed of buildings of an uniform appearance, size, and height. However well proportioned,

B

the gain there might be in dignity would be much more than counterbalanced by the great loss in play of fancy, in light and shade, in poetry, in that large element of the beautiful produced and governed by the law of contrasts; there would be a monotony which would soon become oppressive. A greater calamity, æsthetically considered, could not befall a city, than to be robbed of all its towers, spires, and monuments—the features which give character and nobility.

It would be impossible, within the limits prescribed, to trace the evolution of towers, steeples, and spires, in the architecture of nations, however interesting such a study would be. Suffice it to say, that, from the Tower of Babel—the father of towers—downwards, amongst all nations that had made progress in the arts of civilization, we find towers, varying of course in form and feature with the special genius of the people, and governed like their other architecture by the nature of the country and the extent of their constructional and scientific skill, yet unmistakably testifying to the universal acceptance and interpretation of this natural law.

We find them rising in massive grandeur from the shifting sands of Egypt in pyramidal form; we see them soaring above the myriad population of China, tier upon tier, in their pagoda splendour; they speak to us from India, in the topes which rear their rich and filagreed forms over the country; the storied soil of Italy finds interpretation of its progressive culture, in the towers that fling their long shadows as the sun rises and sets, from the primitive Campanile of Ravenna to the fair Lily of Florence. And, nearer home, our Saxon and Celtic forefathers speak to us across the centuries from the round towers of the Eastern Counties and the Green Isle. Only from classic Greece comes an uncertain sound, and the reason may not be far to seek; for, without encroaching on the realms of fancy, it may be that the constant yearning of mankind for the infinite and the supernatural, found some expression in the rearing of lofty pinnacle and massy tower. Now the Greek religion was essentially a worship of humanity, a system of demonology, a self-satisfied thing, with no yearnings after a nobler divinity, or, if there were, satisfied with the erection of an altar to "an unknown god." A people of high culture and refinement, theirs—as must invariably be in all true architecture—was the natural exponent of their creed. Yet we find that even they had some perception of this truth, as they placed their buildings, when possible, upon eminences to give height and majesty, and raised their Temple of the Winds. The more evident reasons for towers and steeples, however, readily suggest themselves—viz., to give emphasis and importance to a building, to serve as bell towers when bells came into general use, and for purposes of better observation over the country in warlike and troublous times, as well as to serve for landmarks, &c. It must be conceded, however, that the tower in combination with the spire was *par excellence* a creation of the Gothic spirit. Some writers have regarded it as a Christian emblem, and that, piercing the air as it tapered to a point, it symbolized the Church's hope for the future. Although it may be a pleasing sentiment, this was certainly not the origin, for in a spire there is an obvious fitness, and a natural finish to a tower, which commends and recommends itself.

With the Renaissance the idea of adopting what was felt to be a noble architectural feature, and remoulding it in a Classic form, was conceived, many examples of which we find in Spain, Portugal, Italy, and other parts of the Continent; and in Sangallo's clever design for St. Peter's at Rome, made about 1540, he shows two very lofty steeples of good design, but this design was not carried out. These examples, however, do not

appear to have been known in this country, as it must be
remembered that at that time Englishmen were insular, and
little travelled, and illustrated architectural books not much in
vogue ; so that we may fairly ascribe to Sir Christopher Wren
the credit of his steeples as original conceptions: and when
we consider the times, his training, and the difficulties which
surrounded him, we cannot but profoundly admire his achieve-
ments. It may be said that he had an opportunity that comes to
few men to show his capabilities ; and yet, how few men with a
similar opportunity could have taken so noble an advantage of it.
The times were made for the man, and the man for the times.
Providence always raises up some one to be a leader of men,
who shall forge new links on the chain of noble art work,
binding the past to the present, and the present to the future.

While St. Peter's at Rome was receiving its last touches in
the shape of a Baldachino from the hands of Bernini, the
occupants of a quiet rectory house in Wiltshire were hailing
the arrival of a child who was destined to begin, carry on, and
complete a building which is little inferior, and in many respects
even superior, to the great Pontifical Cathedral. His father, who
was afterwards Dean of Windsor, was a man of considerable
attainments both in science and literature ; to these he added
some skill in architecture, and it is curious to find that he was
even employed in the designing of a Royal building. His son,
therefore, who was of a delicate constitution, had the advantage
of his father's tuition, and profited largely thereby. From an
early age young Christopher developed great powers of ingenuity.
When he was only thirteen he invented a new astronomical
instrument; at the age of fourteen he went to Oxford, and
shortly afterwards made an instrument for writing with two pens
simultaneously ; he also largely aided in perfecting the barometer,
if he did not invent it ; and Evelyn says of him at this time,

"After dinner I visited that miracle of a youth, Mr. Christopher Wren." At the age of twenty-five he was chosen Professor of Astronomy at Gresham College, and was one of those who founded the Royal Society. He had early developed a fondness for mathematics, which he had assiduously pursued as a study, and doubtless had also taken up architecture, as not uncommon amongst the gentlemanly accomplishments of the time; but it was more than a pastime to him, for he seems to have studied Vitruvius with all the energy he had brought to bear on his other studies, so much so as to have acquired a reputation at Oxford, although as yet his knowledge was purely theoretical. He was, however, soon to have an opportunity, and in an unexpected manner, of putting his ideas into practice. In 1661, Inigo Jones being dead, and there being no architect of great repute left, the King sent for Wren to assist Sir John Denham, who was then the Surveyor-General of his Majesty's works. In the following year he was requested to survey old St. Paul's, and draw up a scheme for repairing it; for beyond strengthening some portions, and adding his celebrated Western Portico, Inigo Jones had been able to do nothing.

In 1663 Wren's first building was erected, viz., the Sheldonian Theatre at Oxford; then followed the Chapel of Pembroke College; but, feeling probably that he lacked that complete mastery of the artistic element in architecture which he had attained in the scientific, he paid a visit to France, and spent a considerable time in Paris, closely studying all the principal buildings, and especially the Louvre. Writing to a friend at this time he says—"Bernini's design for it I would have given my skin for, but the old Italian only gave me a look at it. . . . I had only time to copy it in my fancy and memory, but shall be able, by discourse and crayon, to give you a tolerable account of it;" and with reference to the other buildings, he writes—"That I might not lose the impressions of these structures I have surveyed, I shall bring you almost all France on paper." He purposed going on to Italy, but was prevented ; and he returned to England in the beginning of 1666.

I have thus far briefly sketched the career of Wren, in order that we may the better understand his works by the light which his early life and training cast upon them.

On the 2nd of September of this year, 1666, the Great Fire began, the history of which is so well-known that it need not be dwelt upon. Suffice it to say, that eighty-seven Parish Churches and six Chapels, together with over twelve thousand houses, were destroyed.

Wren was now to show his capabilities, which were equal to the occasion. There is an old saying, that "Everything cometh in time to him who can wait."—his time had come. Within a few days he had his plan for the rebuilding of the city prepared; and although it was much superior to any of the others, the jealousy and cupidity of private owners prevented the scheme from being executed. Had it been carried out, London would have been the finest city in the world, with wide river quays and a broad rolling river ; its Royal Exchange standing in a large piazza, as the centre from which streets ninety and sixty feet wide were to radiate ; the churches were to be placed in conspicuous, and as far as possible, insular positions ; and all churchyards, and buildings for trade using great fires, were to be put out of town. Thousands of pounds have been spent every year in the buying up of property to widen the streets, and in the loss of time caused by the constant blocking up of the narrow thoroughfares, in expiation of the folly of those citizens.

Sir Christopher Wren was now appointed Deputy Surveyor-General, and principal architect for rebuilding the entire city ; and, Sir John Denham dying in 1668, he succeeded to his office. He set himself resolutely to the work of rebuilding some fifty of the parish churches, together with a new St. Paul's. However interesting it would be to trace the progress of all his works, I must confine myself to his Steeples and Towers, which are in themselves quite worthy of maintaining his reputation. Before enumerating these and examining them in detail, it would be advantageous to endeavour to find out the general principles which governed his conceptions, so far as they can be obtained from himself, or deduced from his works.

From the 'Parentalia' we find that his idea in building his Churches was—"to bring them out as far as possible from the obscure lanes, not too nicely to observe east and west, unless they fall out properly; such fronts as shall lie most open in view should be adorned with porticoes, both for beauty and convenience, which, together with handsome spires or lanterns, rising in good proportions above the neighbouring houses, may be of sufficient ornament to the town without a great expense, for enriching the outward walls of the church in which plainness and duration ought principally to be studied." And specially of the towers he says—"When a parish is divided, I suppose it may be thought sufficient if the mother church has a tower, large enough for a good ring of bells, and the other churches, smaller towers for two or three bells; because great towers and lofty steeples are sometimes more than half the charge of the church."

Examining his steeples and towers, several excellencies which lie on the surface suggest themselves, and others will appear as we proceed to examine them in detail.

First.—Their SCIENTIFIC CONSTRUCTION. Most of them have stood the test of nearly two hundred years, and they are almost as sound and strong to-day as when they were built. Wren took no liberties, and ran no risks; there is no rule-of-thumb work, all his construction is sound and thoroughly scientific. In his reports

on Salisbury Cathedral, and on Westminster Abbey, he blames
their original builders for their daring and risky construction, and
goes on to shew that the central tower of Salisbury is entirely
dependent on its iron bars and straps, and that if these were
removed it would inevitably fall. He took care not to fall into
this mistake, for in only two of his steeples, so far as I am aware,
did he use any iron tie-rods, and the iron chain round the
springing of the dome of St. Paul's is rather precautionary than
really necessary.

Second.—The MATERIALS USED, and the GOOD QUALITY OF
THE WORKMANSHIP. His materials were carefully selected, and all
of the best of their kind; he was too thorough to neglect anything
which would tend to ensure the stability of his work. His axiom
was, "Buildings ought to be eternal." Most of the stone is
Portland, and the timber English oak; he had no patience with
the Caen stone, and the foreign chesnut which he found had
been used at Westminster; the lead is seldom less than 10 lbs.
to the foot, and of much better quality than it is possible to
obtain now. The tower staircases are generally enclosed in one
angle, which is taken off the inner, and do not show on the
outer side, the steps and newals being of stone: the walls are
always of ample thickness, seldom being less than 3 feet thick,
and often more. As of his materials, so of his workmanship, he
was fortunate in gathering round him a body of clever and reliable
artificers; and his master mason, Thomas Strong, seems to have
been skilful and ingenious. Wren overlooked nothing. Writing
when in France to the Master of Trinity College, Cambridge,
with reference to his designs for some additions, he says—"I
suppose you have good masons; however, I would willingly take
further pains to give all the mouldings in great. We are
scrupulous in small matters, and,—you must pardon us,—we
architects are as great pedants as the critics or heralds."

Third.—Their HAPPY PROPORTIONS. Nothing can exceed these, whether the towers are seen in elevation or perspective, with one or two exceptions; and it is remarkable that all his towers would bear lanterns or spires without destroying their proportions; and all the steeples, notably those with lead lanterns and spires, would bear the removal of the upper portions, leaving only the tower part, without detracting from the beauty or proportion of such towers. This is a severe test, and one which many steeples, both Classic and Gothic, could not successfully stand.

Fourth.—Their ARCHITECTURAL FEATURES. The lower stages of the towers are plain, dignified, and solid looking, with small piercings; the storeys are emphasized by stone bands or strings, and a well-designed cornice and parapet, sometimes plain, at other times enriched, appropriately finish the top. It is only in the upper stages that Wren allowed his fancy to riot amid graceful and elegant shapes. We never find the towers poised on the top of a roof, or rising from behind a portico; they generally project slightly from the line of the church, so as to lead the eye from the ground upwards; and Wren thus obtained not only that satisfactory appearance that the eye demands, but also increased their apparent height. We can hardly apply to any of them the just stricture which Professor Blackie applied to an Edinburgh steeple of not ungraceful outline and feature, but which rose from the roof of a plain, round, and very ugly church—"an angel riding on a beer barrel." The happy junctures of towers and spires must not be overlooked. They are rarely clumsy, generally graceful in contour, and often exquisite in a subtle grace of line and curve. This is not a little due to his custom of designing in perspective, a rule which he inculcates strongly in his writings.

The work of a man of genius, indeed of any man, is rarely equal; there are times when he gives birth to conceptions which seem nothing less than inspirations, at other times they hardly reach mediocrity. A man is not always at his best, and there are times when, if he produces work, it must be of an inferior kind; and when work flows in, giving no time for matured thought and study, is it to be wondered at that the standard falls?

Thus it was with Sir Christopher Wren; yet when we consider the amount of work crowded into his life, the wonder is that it was done so well; besides, we do not know what elements of economy, or what pressure of parochial and vestry requirements, were brought to bear upon him. He was not likely altogether to escape that outside pressure which is felt so keenly by many of his brethren in the present day.

And now let us consider in detail his Steeples and Towers, dividing them, for the sake of clearness, into—

    I.   Those in London : (*a*) existing ; (*b*) pulled down.

    II. Those outside of London.

As this is not simply a panegyric on the works of Sir Christopher Wren, but an honest endeavour to consider them in themselves, and in the light of their message to us of to-day, I trust I may not be thought presumptuous, if, in doing so, I venture here and there to find fault, and even suggest alternative modes of treatment where such seem to be desirable.

The existing steeples and towers designed by Wren in London may roughly be divided into the following groups :—

    I. The Stone Steeples, of which there are nine, exclusive of the Campanili of St. Paul's.

    2. The Timber and Lead Spires and Lanterns, of which there are nineteen.

    3. The Towers, of which there are twelve, exclusive of the Western Towers of Westminster Abbey.

· S· Bride· Fleet· St· | · S· Mary· le Bow· Cheapside · | · S· Vedast· Foster· Lane·

·Christ· Ch· Newgate St· | Campanili · S· Paul's· Cath!· | ·S· Dunstan· in· the· East·

I.—THE STONE STEEPLES.

St. Mary-le-Bow, Cheapside.—The space for the old tower had been taken out of the corner of the church, and had stood back some forty feet from the front of the houses. Wren determined to keep his new tower clear of the church, and brought it forward to the street line. In sinking for the foundations, after getting down 18 feet, he came to what turned out to be the old Roman causeway, 4 feet thick, and on this he decided to rear his tower. It measures 32 feet square at the base, and about 122 feet high to the top of the belfry story, and with the steeple rises, according to the most recent measurements, to a total height of 221 ft. 9 in. to top of dragon. It was begun in 1671, and was not finished until 1677, and cost £7388, or nearly as much as the church. The tower is divided into three main stages, the lower-most one contains two enriched doorways under semicircular arches; the next story has a projecting balcony with access to same, and semicircular niches on each side. Over this projects the clock; the belfry stage has two pair of Ionic pilasters on each face, and, in the centre, large circular-headed openings filled in with louvres. Over this is a well designed cornice, with moulded balustrading above, and angle-piers from which rise lofty cartouches surmounted by vases. A circular dome, 20 feet diameter, springing from long moulded corbels, rises about 18 feet, and carries a stone cylinder 11 feet diameter inside, and 9 inches thick; this again is domed over to carry the lantern, and again to carry the small spire at the top. The weight and thrust of the upper portion is very skilfully taken by the inverted trusses, which are really flying buttresses, supported on the circular peristyle of twelve Corinthian columns ; a very beautiful feature, gracefully clothing but not hiding the construction. (See section.) In 1820 the steeple was repaired, and new red granite columns and entablatures fixed at the lantern stage ; the old ones of Portland stone having presumably decayed. The well known dragon crowns the top. There was a prophecy that when this dragon and the grasshopper on the top of the Royal Exchange should meet, serious events were to take place; and, curiously enough, both were being repaired at the same time, and lay in a builder's yard together ;—whether the calamities foretold came to pass, is not said.

The chimes of Bow Bells have rung merrily in many a chronicler's account of old and new London.

There is an indescribable charm about the steeple of St. Mary-le-Bow, which is hardly equalled by any other that I know of ; it has a gracefulness which is full of strength, a subtle play of light and shade which is more akin to the Gothic than the Classic, an abiding beauty which touches our emotions to their deepest depths. One would be bold to criticise it, yet, if such were allowable, we might wish that the diameter of the cylinder behind the beautiful peristyle had been increased, say one foot more in the radius, which would still have left ample space behind the columns, and would have given an appearance of greater solidity to this part, and strength to the whole.

Campanili of St. Paul's Cathedral.—Wren's first design for the new Cathedral shows no western towers, and although in some respects it was better than the one adopted, yet the addition of the towers is a decided gain. They form, with the portico and pediment, a noble western façade. The Campanili rise to a height of 220 feet, and are divided into five stories, two up to cornice of church, and three in the upper portion. The

Pl. 2.

S. Bride
Fleet. St.

S. Mary. le. Bow
. Cheapside.

F · · F

E

E

E

D

C

B

A

F · · F

E

E

D

C

B

A

C · · D

A · · B

C · · D

A · · B

lowermost stage has coupled Corinthian pilasters, and deeply recessed windows; the next has similar pilasters, but of the Composite order, with square-headed windows, having columns, entablature, and pediment; over this is the clock story, the aperture for which is blank in the north campanile; this is flanked by groups of sculpture at the angles; above, the next story rises circular, pierced with four openings, and having projecting angular coupled columns and entablature crowned by vases. Eight openings pierce the next story divided by piers at angles, and from the upper stage rises a double-ogee curved roof terminating in gilded pine-apple shaped finials.

Any description, however, gives no idea of the grace and beauty of the whole, the subtle contrast of lines, and play of light and shade, which must be seen to be understood.

The south tower contains the clock and great bell, and the well-known Geometrical Staircase. In the north tower has recently been hung a small carillon of bells, and it is noteworthy that the tower had been designed with such forethought that no structural alterations were required to be made.

They are amongst the finest of Wren's compositions, and were it not that they are overshadowed by the noble dome, could not fail to be more appreciated.

St. Bride, or St. Bridget, Fleet Street, is one of Wren's most noteworthy steeples, and is original in its construction. It was erected in 1680, and measures 30 feet at the base: it rose originally to a height of 234 feet, but having been struck by lightning, was reduced 8 feet.

The steeple is carried on a flat, ogee-shaped dome, about 17 feet diameter at spring, and rising 14 feet, inside measurements; a circular moulding runs round the springing, and this is brought to the square by plain pendentives. From this the steeple rises in ever lessening stages round the central staircase, until the spire, with sides concave in plan, crowns the whole. The first three storeys above the belfry stage are constructed on a plan, roughly speaking, like a wheel, with the centre newal of the staircase as the axle, and the divisions pierced by arched apertures running to each angle of the octagon as the spokes. This gives great strength, the arrangement forming a series of cells. (See illustrations.) The upper stages are of the ordinary octagonal form.

The proportion and poise of this steeple is exceedingly good, and from almost any point piles well; but one tires of the repetition of stage after stage, only varied by receding in width and height, and slightly in detail, suggesting, as some one has said, the prosaic lines of a drawn-out telescope, and the fear that it will suddenly collapse when least expected. There is not the fancy, nor the play of light and shade, that we find in St. Mary-le-Bow,— it is blank verse, to the rhythm and cadence of the other; or, as it were, the child of Wren's mathemetical knowledge, as contrasted with that knowledge draped in artistic garb which is displayed in the other.

St. Vedast, Foster Lane, one of the best known by name, at the present time, of any of the City steeples, was erected in 1697. It is considerably less in bulk than the preceding ones, the tower being only 20 feet square, and the total height about 160 feet. It is, however, exceedingly pleasing in contour and line, although it is perhaps one of the simplest of all Wren's steeples, and on analysis you almost wonder wherein the charm consists; there is little of the light and shade of St. Mary-le-Bow, and none of the complicated construction of St. Bride's, and its fenestration is almost common-place; but yet, by reason of its good proportions, and notably its play of curved lines—concave on the lower stage

Pl. 3.

Christ · Church ·
· Newgate · St ·

S. Vedast ·
· Foster Lane ·

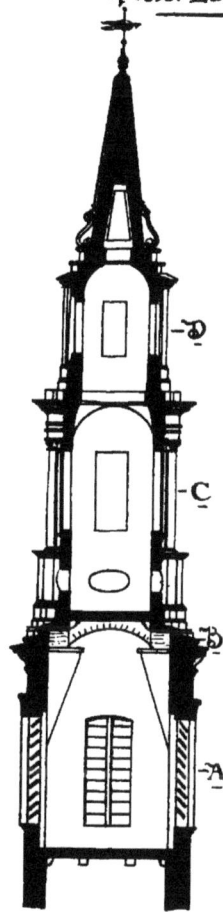

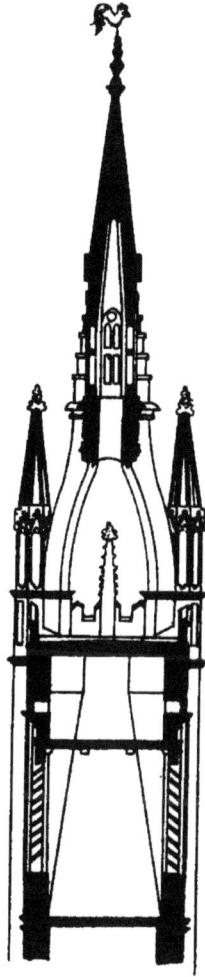

S. Dunstan · in · the · East ·
· S. Dunstan's Hill ·

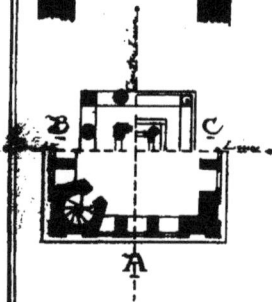

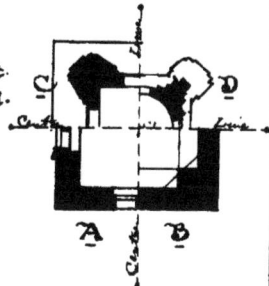

of the steeple, convex on the upper, the spire also assuming an appearance of concavity from the projecting angles—it never fails to please.

Christ Church, Newgate Street, was finished in 1704. It measures 23 feet at base, and reaches the same altitude as St. Vedast ; its construction, however, is much more intricate. Squinches contract the square tower to the octagon, and support four arches, from which springs a dome rising about 15 ft. to the crown, and carrying the lantern, the square colonnade standing partly upon the haunch of the dome, and partly on the arches. The lowermost stage of the tower is open on three sides, with arched openings : the belfry stage with its triple openings and flat pilasters is very beautiful; but, as seen from the front of St. Sepulchre's Church, or on the angle, the stages above appear to contract too suddenly, and the gradation does not seem so happy as usual. Had the vases, which now stand on the centre of the cumbered pediments, been placed at the angles instead, as in other examples, I venture to think the contour would have been more satisfactory.

St. Dunstan in the East, St. Dunstan's Hill, is a good example of how Wren caught the Gothic feeling, without having the knowledge of detail necessary for carrying it out with purity. This is probably one of those he refers to in his Report on Westminster Abbey, accompanying his design for new towers, &c. in which he says—" They may agree with the original scheme of the old architects, without any modern mixtures to show my own inventions : in like manner as J have among the parochial churches of London given some few examples (when I was obliged to deviate from a better style), which appear not ungraceful, but ornamental to the east part of the City."

It was built in 1698; and as seen from the foot of St. Dunstan's Hill is extremely well proportioned, light, and graceful. The tower is 21 feet square at base, and rises with the steeple to a height of 167 feet; it consists of four stories, including the clock stage; from each angle rises a tall pinnacle, and from behind springs a flying buttress, to support a lantern 6 feet across and about 49 feet high. The thrust of these buttresses is taken by long flat pendentives in the angles, 32 feet long, measured from the flat roof (see accompanying section), and reaching down to the belfry floor. Although fragile looking to an ordinary observer, it is perhaps one of Wren's strongest steeples; such faith had he in it, that it is said, on being told that a hurricane had damaged all the steeples in London, he exclaimed—"Not St. Dunstan's, I am sure!"

On comparing it with similar steeples which we possess in this country, viz. St. Nicholas, Newcastle, St. Giles, Edinburgh, and King's College, Old Aberdeen, it is difficult to agree with those who laud it as much superior to any of these. Even its scientific construction is perhaps overpraised, because, with the thrust taken so far down into the tower, it becomes almost entirely a perpendicular weight. Then again, its details are such a travesty of the Gothic that they go far to destroy the pleasure that its general outline gives us. The fenestration of the lantern is effective, but beyond this the design of this portion is almost commonplace, as evidenced in the finishing of the flying buttresses at the top with a series of steps, a feature, however, which Wren often used. It follows closer upon the lines of St. Nicholas, Newcastle, than either of the others, they having the baronial features which characterized the Scotch Gothic of that period, and there is a sturdiness and strength about St. Giles, Edinburgh, especially, to which St. Dunstan's makes no claim. It shows, however, the boldness of Wren's genius, that he

Pl. 4.

S. Michael · College Hill ·   S. Stephen · Walbrook ·   S. James · Garlick · Hill ·

S. Mary · Magdalene ·   *Old Fish St.*   S. Magnus · London · Br · ·   S. Margaret · Pattens · · Rood Lane ·

fearlessly essayed to build a steeple of a form which could only be carried out in a style foreign to him ; but he seems ever to have delighted in making difficulties, in order that he might overcome them.

St. Michael Royal and St. Martin Vintry, College Hill.— The church was rebuilt in 1694, but the steeple was not completed until 1713. It measures 20 ft. 6 in. at base, and rises to a height of 128 feet. This is one of three which are modelled on the same lines, although possessing each their individuality,— the others being St. James, Garlick Hill, and St. Stephen's, Walbrook.

The tower consists of three stories; the lowermost one is pierced by a circular-headed window, with architraves and keystones, upon which cherubs' heads are carved; the next story has a circular window ; and the top, or belfry stage, square openings, with moulded architrave round, and cornice along top ; the openings are divided by a plain stone mullion, and filled in with louvres. A cornice, with consoles surmounted by a pierced parapet, with angle and centre piers—the former supporting vases—crowns the tower. The steeple rises in a circular form, from a shallow dome supported by four arches, springing from plain pendentives (see section), the inner core being octagonal, with angle piers, and pierced on each face and surrounded by a beautiful circular colonnade of eight Ionic columns. Over this rises an octagonal stage with angle trusses, and the steeple terminates with a solid pedestal, finial, and vane. The steeple *per se* is very beautiful, and, seen on elevation, makes with the tower an exceedingly well-balanced composition ; but, seen diagonally, the tower being square and of considerable width, and the steeple being circular, and then octagonal, there is nothing to lead the eye from the one to the other ; accordingly

C

the upper portion appears too narrow for the lower, and detracts from the otherwise beautiful composition.

St. Stephen, Walbrook, was probably not finished until 1681. It measures 20 feet at the base, and rises to a total height of about 130 feet. The tower consists of four stories; the first and second have square windows, and architraves round, with cornice over; the third has a plain circular window; and the top or belfry story has a circular-headed opening on each face, with moulded architrave round, and filled in with louvres. An enriched cornice, designed with great feeling, over which rises an open moulded balustrade, with small piers at centre and angles, completes the tower externally. Internally, a shallow dome springs from four arches at the level of cornice to carry steeple, which consists of two main stories, square-shaped, with wide open apertures on each face; the lower story has three clustered columns, with entablature at each angle, surmounted by vases; the upper story has a panelled projecting pier at each angle, surmounted by balls. Above rises a solid moulded and panelled spirelet, finishing with a finial and vane; the staircase, as usual, is in the angle, not visible on the outside, except by narrow slits for light. The steeple is very light and graceful, but perhaps too light and open for the tower, which is unusually sombre and heavy. It is doubtful what Wren intended by his tower,—I hardly think he intended it to appear as it now does—"skinned," but rather that his intention was to have the face cemented, for the stone-walling is rough, and there are no quoins such as we find almost invariably in his other towers. The probability is that the tower was so hemmed in by adjoining houses at the time it was built, that only the upper portion of it could be seen, so that he lavished all his care on that portion, to the exclusion of the lower.

Pl. 5.

S. Mary. Magdalene
Old. Fish St.

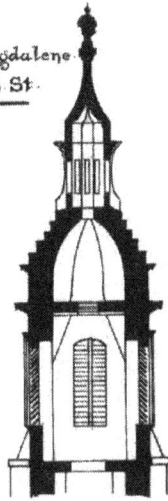

S. James
Garlick Hill

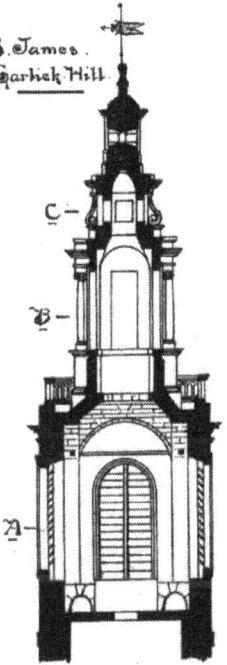

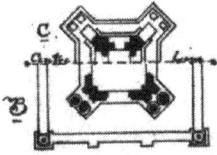

S. Michael.
College Hill.

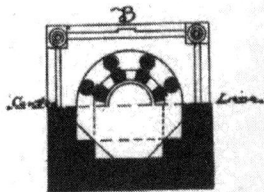

S. Stephen.
Walbrook

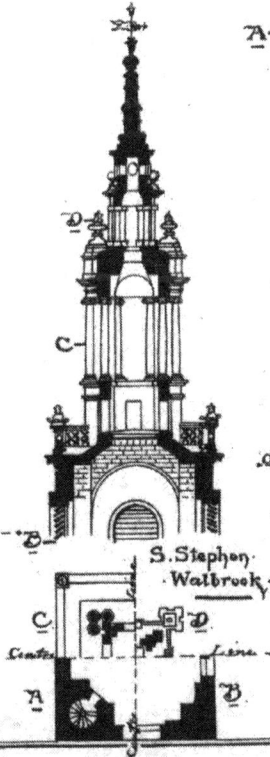

St. James, Garlick Hill, was erected in 1683. It measures 20 feet at base, and rises to a height of about 125 feet. The tower is divided into three stories; the lowermost story contains a doorway, with Corinthian column, entablature, and pediment; the second story, a round window, with pediment, and circular, blank clock face over; and the top, or belfry stage, is pierced by circular-headed openings filled in with louvres. A cornice, with a fenestrated parapet, and angle-piers supporting vases, complete the tower externally. Internally, a shallow dome springing from four arches (the angle-piers of which go down to belfry floor, and are carried on squinches) supports the steeple or lantern, which is again arched over to carry the upper portions. (See section.) The steeple is square, with openings on each face, having projecting coupled columns set anglewise, and vases and trusses over; these widen out the upper portion, and, although not so beautiful in itself as St. Michael's, College Hill, yet, by reason of these angles, the general contour, viewed diagonally, is better.

A projecting clock, supported by a carved bracket, and having a curious figure—possibly intended for St. James—over it, is a noticeable feature, but this is comparatively modern.

St. Mary Magdalen and St. Gregory by St. Paul, Old Fish Street, was erected in 1685, and is a small steeple, being only 86 feet high. It is very unpretending: its general effect, however, is pleasing. From the belfry stage of the tower rises an octagonal dome, 9 feet diameter, and rising 10 feet, inside measurement; this is brought to the square by a plain pendentive. The outside of the dome recedes by regular steps, from which rises a simple stone lantern, pierced by narrow openings, and surmounted by a cornice and small concave spirelet, finishing with a vase.

II.—THE LEAD SPIRES AND LANTERNS.

St. Magnus, London Bridge, first claims attention, as being a compromise between a stone steeple and a lead lantern. It was erected in 1705, and is well proportioned and pleasing in outline, rising to a height of 185 feet. It measures one foot longer north and south than it does east and west.

The tower is three stories to the top of parapet, from which rises an octagonal stone lantern of the Composite order, covered with a lead cupola, which again bears a small timber and lead lantern and spire; the square tower is contracted to the octagon by moulded corbelling. The ground story is open on three sides, the fourth being the entrance to the church, and is similar in this respect to Christ Church, Newgate. It was not originally so, but the arches were opened out, after the fire of 1759, to form the footway to old London Bridge, when it was found that Wren had made provision for this possibility, foreseeing that the increased traffic over the old bridge, which crossed the river at this point, would necessitate it sooner or later. When the present London Bridge was built, in 1830, this tower of St. Magnus, which was formerly in the stream of traffic, was left in the eddy, and now stands in the undisturbed repose of the churchyard. The western face of this ground story is open to objection, in that it has all the members—pilasters, entablature, and pediment—of an Ionic portico; beautiful in itself, but interfering with what is so pleasing in most of his towers, the rising straight from the ground. One cannot get rid of the feeling that it is standing on the top of a pediment. The plate-tracery balustrade over tower cornice has also a rather thin and weak appearance, and hardly consorts with the solid-looking tower, the compact lantern, and the full swelling cupola ; but these are as "spots in the sun" in this fine composition, which stands out prominent in the second rank of Wren's creations.

It will be appropriate to take the Lead Spires, pure and simple, first, of which there are two, viz. St. Margaret Pattens, and St. Swithin's.

St. Margaret Pattens, Rood Lane, was erected in 1687. It measures 22 feet square at the base, and rises to a height of 200 feet, and is the highest of all the lead spires or lanterns.

The tower rises three stories above the parapet of the church, with flat pilasters at the angles, and is finished by a bold cornice surmounted by a balustrade of square moulded balusters and angle piers, on which stand tall obelisk pinnacles. From within the balustrade springs a tall octagonal lead spire, panelled on each face in the height, pierced by small openings, and terminating in a vane. The spire timbering is skilfully framed and disposed, and springing well from the tower, and strongly braced. The tower and spire are well proportioned, shewing that Wren, when he chose, could adopt the simple Gothic spire form, and translate it into Classic without loss of grace or power, although his sympathies were evidently with more sensuous forms ; and so we find, when the spire was taken as a basis, his exuberant fancy breaking out into a concave outline as in St. Nicholas Cole-abbey, or beginning with a domical form as in St. Peter's, Cornhill, or with an ogee as in St. Martin's, Ludgate.

St. Swithin, Cannon Street, was erected in 1679. It measures 20 feet at base, and rises to a height of 150 feet. The timber construction of the spire is extremely simple, and springs directly from the top of the octagon. (See section.) The device employed to bring the square tower into the octagon is not a very happy one, viz., a large scooped-out splay, round which a well-designed enriched cornice and balustrade run. On elevation the lines are good, but the diagonal view brings the splays into almost painful obtrusiveness. Had some such arrangement been adopted as at St. Martin's, Ludgate, I cannot but think it would have been more satisfactory.

We will now take the other Lanterns in their alphabetical order.

St. Anne and St. Agnes cum St. John Zachary, St. Anne's Lane, Aldersgate. In pursuit of our subject we find that sometimes the steeple is noble and the church ignoble; sometimes the steeple and the church are alike noble; in other cases the church is pleasing and the steeple or tower commonplace. This is one of the latter class. It was erected in 1680; is 14 feet square at base, and measures 95 feet to top of vane of lantern. It is built of brick cemented on face, with stone quoins, and finished with a plain unpierced parapet. A small wooden lantern rises from the flat roof, with an ogee top, surmounted by a vane bearing the letter A.

St. Augustine and St. Faith, Watling Street, was erected in 1695, and is 20 feet square at base, and rises to a height of 140 feet. The tower rises two stories above the parapet of the church. The lower one is relieved by a small circular window, the upper or belfry stage by a square opening surrounded by an architrave, and filled in with louvres; an enriched cornice, and fenestrated parapet of good design, with angle-piers forming bases for tall

Pl. 6.

S. Swithin Cannon St.

S. Augustine & S. Faith
Watling St.

S. Anne & S. Agnes.
St Annes Lane

S. Benet Pauls Wharf

S. Edmund the King.
Lombard St.

S. James Westminster
Piccadilly

obelisk-shaped pinnacles, complete the tower. From this rises a tall lantern of two stories, with angle buttresses, and on top a tall spire terminating in a vane. There is considerable fancy displayed here, but the upper and the lower portions hardly appear to be well balanced, the lantern having the appearance of being too high and attenuated for the tower.

St. Benet and St. Peter, Paul's Wharf, was erected in 1683, and is built of brick, with alternate quoins of brick and stone ; it measures 16 feet square at base, and rises to a height of 115 feet. The tower is exceedingly plain, with square openings at belfry stage, filled in with louvres, and finished with a heavy enriched cornice and blocking course, from which rises a lead cupola, with small oval apertures, and an open lantern on top terminating with a vane. The whole is unassuming, but of good and pleasing proportions.

St. Edmund the King and St. Nicholas Acons, Lombard Street, was erected in 1690; measures 17 feet square at base, and rises to a height of 136 feet. The tower is of three stories ; ground floor containing a square-headed door with projecting cornice ; the second story has a circular-headed window with cornice and pediment over, the full width of tower ; over this window projects the clock ; the top or belfry story has a circular-headed window filled in with louvres. This story is blended with the parapet of church by large curved consoles or brackets on each side. A good cornice with consoles, and a dead panelled parapet, with angle and centre piers, complete the tower ; on the angle-piers stand vases, and on the centre ones pineapples. From this rises a well-proportioned lead octagonal lantern, with angle-piers and brackets supporting the cornice, and ornamented with lighted urns or flaming torches at each angle, emblematical of the Great Fire ; above rises a concave octagonal spire, terminating in a well-pronounced pedestal supporting a finial and vane. The outline of tower and lantern is exceedingly pleasing.

St. James, Westminster.—This might be put in the same category as that of St. Anne and St. Agnes. The tower is of brick, with no special features, and surmounted by a cornice and balustrade. A lantern springs from the flat roof, but is so commonplace and ignoble that it is quite unworthy of the church and situation.

St. Lawrence Jewry, Guildhall, was erected in 1667; measures 25 feet square at base, and rises to a total height of 160 feet, inclusive of vane. The tower consists of three main stories : the lowermost one contains a doorway, with cornice and pediment over, supported on consoles; the second stage is very simple, and is only broken by a small window with a segmental arch; the upper or belfry stage has angle-piers, and each face is pierced by a large aperture filled in with louvres : in the heads of two of these are clock dials. An enriched, cornice, with moulded balusters over, and angle-piers supporting tall obelisks terminating in balls, surmount the tower. Above rises a square turret, or lantern, with projecting cornice and pediment, and a circular-headed louvred opening in each face; on this is set a square pedestal, from which rises an octagonal spirelet, terminating in a large ball and vane, bearing the gridiron, as representing the mode of St. Lawrence's martyrdom. The composition is more vigorous than refined, but pleasing withal, not so much from the multiplicity of lines, as from the simplicity and strength of the composition.

Pl. 7.

S. Margaret · Lothbury ·

S. Lawrence · Jewry · Guild⁴ ·

S. Martin · Ludgate ·

S. Mary · Abchurch ·

S. Mary · Aldermanbury ·

S. Michael · Bassishaw ·
Basinghall St.

St. Margaret, Lothbury, was erected in 1690; measures 18 feet at base, and rises to a total height of 140 feet. The tower is divided into three stories: the lowermost one contains a square-headed door, flanked by detached Corinthian columns supporting entablature and pediment; the second story is pierced by a circular-headed window with moulded architrave round, and double festoon of carved flowers and fruit over; the third, or belfry story, has openings with segmental arched heads divided by stone mullions, and filled in with louvres. A plain cornice and blocking course complete the tower, from which rises a lead-covered square, cupola-shaped, lantern, pierced with small apertures, with lower and upper mouldings, and from this springs a tall panelled obelisk, with balls under the lower angles, terminating with finial and vane.

The tower is graceful and well-proportioned, and the whole composition is inoffensive and quiet, but the lantern does not merit great praise—it too strongly suggests the simple lines of an extinguisher, and hardly gives the impression of much thought having been bestowed upon it.

St. Martin, Ludgate, was erected in 1684, and is of the Tuscan order; the tower measures 22 feet at the base, and rises to a height of 158 feet to top of spire. The timber construction is good. (See section.) The tower consists of three stories: in the lowermost story is a doorway with a segmental arch; the second story is pierced by a window with cornice over supported on consoles; above this is a pedimented panel, with festoons of fruit below; the top, or belfry stage, has a large circular-headed opening in each face, with architrave round, filled in with louvres, and a double festoon of carved flowers and fruit over. An enriched cornice crowns the tower; above, the square is reduced externally to the octagon by trusses (see sketch), and internally by squinches. From this springs an ogee roof, covered with lead and pierced with small apertures, which bears a lantern with openings on each face, round the base of which runs a balcony and railing. A spire crowns the whole, springing with angle trusses at the base, and terminating with a vane. A staircase winds round the centre, giving access to balcony. One almost wishes the two immense carved and panelled consoles, at each side of tower, could be removed : they have a thin and sham appearance, and detract from the apparent height of the tower.

St. Mary Abchurch with St. Lawrence Pountney, was erected in 1686 ; measures 20 feet square at base, and rises to a total height of about 140 feet, exclusive of vane. The tower is of brick, with Portland stone quoins and dressings, and is divided into four stories. The first, a ground story, contains a round-headed door, with square cornice over; the second story is relieved by a circular-headed window, and the third story by a circular window, both of which are at present boarded up. The top or belfry stage has a circular-headed window, with carved masks on keystone on each face, and filled in with louvres. A plain cornice completes the tower; from this springs an ogee cupola, supporting a plain lantern and spire, terminating with a vane.

This can hardly be considered one of Wren's successes : probably the pressure of other engagements prevented his personal attention, and it may have been the work of a subordinate.

St. Mary, Aldermanbury, was erected in 1677. It is a well proportioned stone tower, with raised quoins, and large belfry openings. The tower is crowned by a cornice, and parapet partially fenestrated, with bold and not very refined angle

Pl. 8.

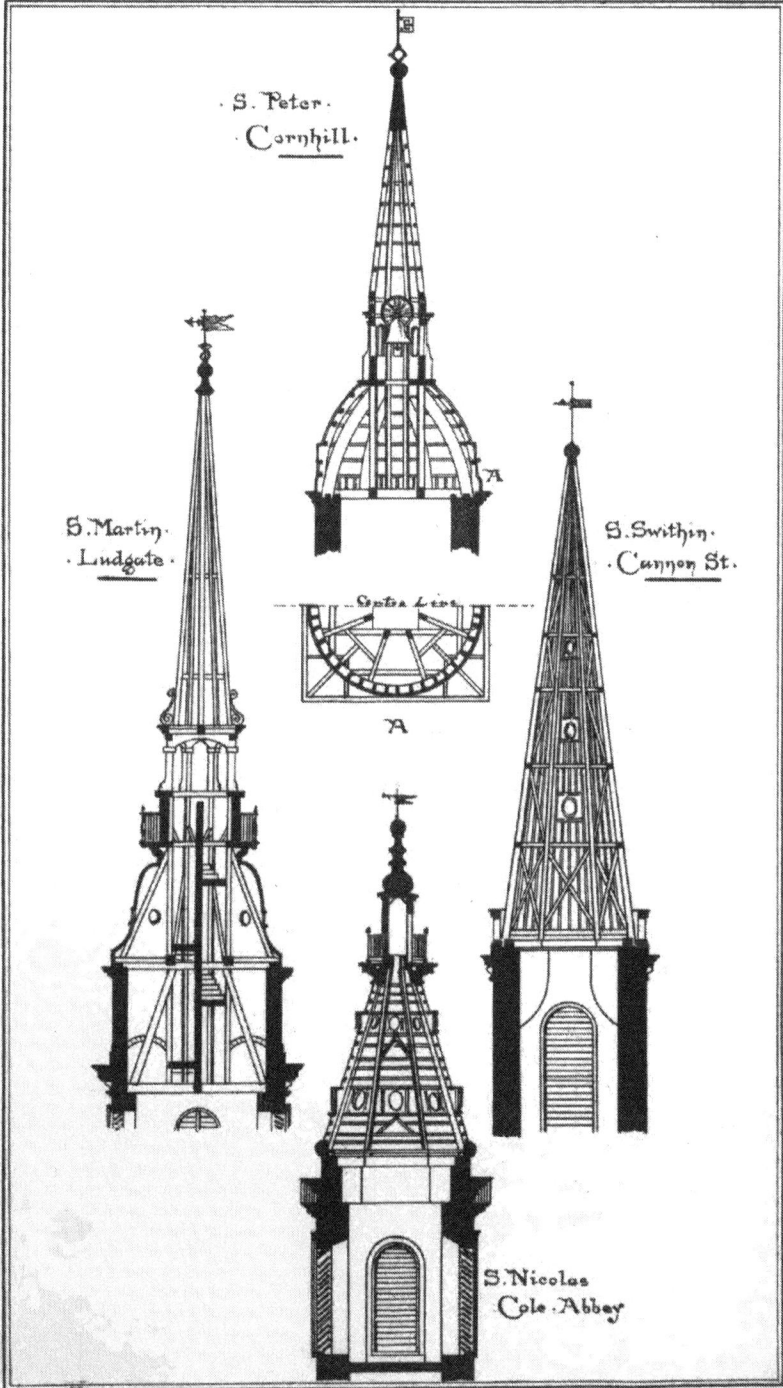

· S. Peter ·
Cornhill ·

· S. Martin ·
· Ludgate ·

· S. Swithin ·
· Cannon St. ·

A

Centre Line

A

S. Nicolas
Cole · Abbey

ornaments. A square turret or lantern of good proportions rises from the flat roof, with clock faces on the lower stage, and having the upper stage boldly pierced with circular-headed openings, and wooden handrails and balustrades; a concave pointed roof, terminating with a vane, surmounts the whole. Like the church, the tower openings have been filled in with Lombardesque tracery, &c., probably about 1820, but which has not improved Wren's work.

St. Michael Bassishaw, Basinghall Street, was erected in 1676; measures 21 feet at base, and rises to a total height of 140 feet. The tower consists of four stories, and is now cemented on face from top to bottom, with the exception of the angle-piers and window dressings, which are of stone. The first and third stories have circular-headed windows; the second is pierced by a round window, and the top or belfry stage has segmental arched openings with moulded architraves round, and filled in with louvres. Narrow slits at south-west angle light the internal staircase. A cornice and dead parapet, with angle-piers supporting pineapple-shaped ornaments, crown the tower. From within the parapet rises a lead lantern with eight sides, the four square sides being greater than the angles : apertures pierce four sides, and buttresses strengthen the angle. A concave-shaped spirelet, with vane, surmounts the whole.

St. Michael, Wood Street, and St. Mary Staining. — The church was erected in 1675. The tower is apparently the old Gothic one, spared from the fire, and repaired by Wren; the middle stage of the tower is adorned by a circular window, with Classic architrave encircling it. Nothing of the original Gothic, however, of any interest remains, and the face of the tower is now

cemented or stuccoed over. A plain stone parapet completes
the tower. A narrow timbered spire, covered with lead, and
peculiarly shaped, rises well within the parapets, terminating in
a vane.

St. Mildred, Bread Street, was erected in 1683; measures
18 feet at the base, and rises to a height of 140 feet, exclusive of
vane. It is now so entirely shut in by tall warehouses, that only
the upper portion of the spire can be seen from below. The
tower, which is of brick, is plain, with circular-headed belfry
openings filled in with louvres. An enriched cornice and
blocking-course caps the tower, from whence springs a pyramidal-
shaped roof covered with lead, and supporting a square lantern
with wide apertures; over this, from a moulded cornice, rises a
slender square spire, terminating with a vane.

St. Nicholas Coleabbey, Fish Street, was erected in 1677;
measures 19 feet at the base, and rises to a height of about
120 feet exclusive of vane. The tower is divided into four stories:
in the lowermost one is a square-headed doorway with cornice
over supported on consoles; the second story is pierced by a
circular window; the third story has a small window, with
cambered pediment over; the top or belfry stage has a circular-
headed opening in each face, surrounded by a square moulded
architrave, and filled in with louvres. An elegant cornice, rising
into a pediment over the belfry openings, and high blocking-
course, with urns at the angles, from which flames are issuing,
complete the tower. From this, with a large bead, springs an
octagonal lead-covered concave spire, pierced with a double row
of elliptical openings, and surmounted by a boldly projecting
cornice forming a balcony, protected by a railing round a square
pedestal, supporting a moulded finial bearing a large gilt ball and

Pl. 9.

S. Mildred. Bread St. | S. Nicholas. Cole. Abbey | S. Stephen. Coleman St.

S. Peter. Cornhill. | S. Alban. Wood St. | S. Andrew in the Wardrobe. Queen Victoria St

vane. The whole composition is very pleasing in its proportions and lines, and bears some resemblance to St. Edmund's, Lombard Street; but it is to be regretted that Wren had not devised some other method of finishing the top of the spire than by a useless balcony, to which it is almost impossible to ascend, as the internal space is so narrow. Something of the same idea is worked out at St. Martin's, Ludgate, but there the balcony is lower down, and is sufficiently wide for easy access.

St. Peter, Cornhill, was erected in 1681; measures 20 feet square at base, and rises to a height of 140 feet. The tower is of brick, well-proportioned, and correct in detail; the belfry stage having a pleasing arcade of triple openings on each face, and finished by a cornice and blocking-course, from which rises a small dome or cupola, covered with lead, and surmounted by an octagonal lantern pierced on each side, from whence springs a spire terminating in a vane in the form of a colossal key of St. Peter. The timber construction is shown on section and plan.

St. Stephen, Coleman Street, was erected in 1676; measures about 65 feet to top of tower, and the lantern about 20 feet more. An elegant cornice with consoles, with a plain parapet over, crowns the tower. From the flat roof within the parapet rises a square bell turret or lantern, with a sloping base, and having a circular-headed opening on each face, with impost, moulding, and cornice and pediment over, from which rises a square concave spirelet, finished by a vane bearing a gilt cock.

III.—TOWERS.

St. Alban, Wood Street, was erected in 1685. It is said that Inigo Jones had rebuilt the church a few years previous to his death. The tower rises to a height of 85 feet, or to top of pinnacles 92 feet, and is finished by an arcaded and panelled open parapet, and crocketted pinnacles, which, having been found to be in a decayed and dangerous state, were replaced about two years ago by new stone. The fenestration of the tower is exceedingly good, and it is well-proportioned and simple in treatment. There is a refinement, and absence of fussiness, which is extremely pleasing, and the details are better than in some others of Wren's Gothic compositions.

All Hallows, Lombard Street, was erected in 1694; measures 21 feet at base, and rises to a height of about 85 feet. It is of stone, and exceedingly plain, and consists of three stories, having on the ground story an entrance doorway with projecting Corinthian columns, and cornice with small square block and pediment over for an inscription. A circular-headed window relieves the second story, the belfry stage being filled in with square louvred openings, surmounted by a cornice. The tower finishes with a plain cornice and high parapet, the upper portion of which is arcaded in pierced plate-tracery work. This, although rather thin and weak-looking, is better in design than some others of a similar kind.

Pl. 10.

Allhallows · Lombard St.   S. Andrew · Holborn.   S. Bartholomew · Moor Lane

S. Clement · S. Clement's Lane   S. Mary · Somerset · Upper Thames St.   S. George · Botolph · Lane.

St. Andrew by the Wardrobe, now in Queen Victoria Street, was erected in 1692; measures 16 feet square at base, and rises to a height of about 86 feet to the top of pinnacles. It is built of brick, with stone dressings and quoins, and, standing as it now does considerably above the level of the street, thus obtains additional height and appearance. It is divided into four stages: the lowermost one is pierced with a small window; the second story has circular-headed windows corresponding with those of the church; the third is taken up with a well-designed clock-case and clock, and the belfry stage has tall square-headed openings filled in with louvres. Piers are carried up the angles of tower, and the whole is finished by a cornice and open balustrading, with angle-piers supporting wrought iron finials. The whole is well-proportioned, and had the angle-piers been treated as pilasters, and furnished with suitable capitals and bases, I am inclined to think they would have given additional elegance, and made it a very pleasing composition. The iron finials or vanes upon the angle-piers are modern additions, and were not intended by Wren.

St. Andrew, Holborn.—The old Gothic tower was not destroyed by the Great Fire, but in 1704 was repaired and refaced with stone, and Classicized by Wren. The tower now measures 23 feet square at base, and rises to a total height of 110 feet. It consists of four stories, including the clock stage, and is covered by a flat lead roof. The belfry openings are more elaborate and intricate in design than usual, but the double arches,—the lower one segmental and the upper one circular,—can hardly be considered a happy or satisfactory arrangement. The tower finishes with a bold cornice supported on consoles, with an open balustrade and piers at each angle, supporting cartouches bearing vanes.

St. Bartholomew, Exchange, formerly in Bartholomew Lane. The church was rebuilt in 1679; the old tower, however, was then standing, and must have been pulled down at a later date. The site having become very valuable, the church and tower were taken down in recent times, and re-erected in Moor Lane, Fore Street, under the direction of Professor Cockerell, and is now called St. Bartholomew, Cripplegate. The tower is in four stages, and surmounted by a curious and eccentric circular-headed doorway rising from the parapet on each face. If the visitor who has climbed to the top yields to the tempting invitation to step out, he will probably find his next step 80 feet lower than the previous one! The tower is commonplace, and the top so ridiculous, that I can hardly think Wren designed it. Although ascribed to him, it was probably done by some one after Wren's time.

St. Clement and St. Martin Orgar, St. Clement's Lane, erected in 1686, measures 16 feet at base, and rises to a height of about 88 feet. It is built of brick, with stone dressings, but is now entirely cemented on the face, with raised quoins. It is divided into three main stages; the lowermost one contains a circular-headed window, with a shallow recess above; the second stage has a circular window, with a stone moulded architrave round; the belfry stage has square openings, divided by plain mullions, and enriched by a moulded architrave and cornice on top, and filled in with louvres. The tower is completed by a cornice supported by consoles, and surmounted by elegant moulded balusters forming an open balustrade, with angle and centre piers, and the whole is simple and in good taste.

St. George, Botolph Lane, was erected in 1674; measures 16 feet at base, and rises to a height of about 84 feet to top of vases.

The tower is of ashlar, well proportioned, and pleasing in outline
and feature, and, amongst the simpler class of towers, is one of
Wren's best. It consists of three stages: the lowermost one is
occupied by the doorway, with a panel above; the second stage
has a circular-headed glazed window, with square cornice over; the
belfry stage is pierced by square openings filled in with louvres.
A plain yet elegant cornice, and dead panelled parapet, with
angle piers supporting vases, veils the lead roof, and crowns the
whole.

St. Mary Aldermary, Bow Lane, was damaged by the Great
Fire, and was repaired, and the upper portion rebuilt and
heightened, by Wren. It measures 24 feet at base, and rises to a
height of 135 feet to top of pinnacles. Wren does not appear to
have displayed his originality here,— the tower having been
carried up on the lines and with the features of the old, except
the pinnacles, and these are rather commonplace. The contour
of the tower is graceful, and the proportions slender, but there
is a monotonous repetition of detail which is disappointing upon
examination.

St. Mary-at-Hill, and St. Andrew Hubbard.—The church was
erected by Wren about 1672, and is an extremely interesting one;
but the old stone tower of the original structure escaped the Great
Fire, and stood until about 1780, when, having become dangerous,
or supposed to be, it was taken down, and the present ugly brick
tower erected.

St. Mary Somerset, Upper Thames Street, erected in 1695.
The church has been pulled down, but, fortunately, ruthless hands
hesitated at the tower, and it still stands, a memorial of the

D

church. It measures 20 feet at base, and rises to a height of
120 feet to top of obelisks. It is divided into five stories
externally, having on the ground story the door with an elliptical
cornice over; round windows on the second; circular-headed
louvred openings on the third; the fourth is similar to the second;
and the belfry story is pierced with circular-headed openings,
with carved grotesque heads on the keystones, and filled in with
louvres. A bold cornice, with carvings over each belfry opening,
and a plain parapet, crowns the tower; high panelled pedestals or
piers rise at the angles and centres of the sides, the angle ones
supporting tall elegant vases, and the centre ones very tall
obelisks panelled on faces, and finished with balls on top, and
angle crockets at bases and centres of each.

St. Matthew, Friday Street.—Erected 1685, and rises to a
height of 74 feet. It is built of brick, in three stages; the upper
one only being emphasized by a plain square belfry window.
It possesses no architectural features whatever, and there is little
doubt that it was not designed by Wren, although generally
included amongst his works. There is a scheme mooted for
pulling both tower and church down, and incorporating the parish
with that of St. Vedast, Foster Lane.

St. Michael, Cornhill, was erected in 1722, although the
church was rebuilt in 1679. It measures 25 feet at base, and
rises to a height of 130 feet to top of pinnacles. It is designed
on the model of the tower of Magdalen College, Oxford.

The conception is very noble, and the spirit of the original
has been successfully caught. There is a solidity and dignity
about it, as well as good proportion, which is impressive.
One regrets that on examination the details do not satisfy,

Pl. 11.

S. Michael Cornhill. | S. Mary Aldermary. Bow Lane. | Westminster Abbey.

S. Olave Jewry. Old Jewry. | Christ Church Oxford. College. | S. Mary Warwick.

more especially as a little closer study of Magdalen Tower would have remedied this defect; but Wren, sharing in the universal contempt in which all things Gothic were held at this time, hardly thought it necessary to follow the style implicitly, preferring rather to give it a Classic tinge. Nevertheless, in spite of these defects, it is superior to its older rival, the tower of St. Sepulchre's, although the latter be more correct in detail. When contrasted with the fussy modern Gothic porch which has recently been added, the conparison but serves to suggest Landseer's well-known picture of " Dignity and Impudence."

The tower consists of three main stages, with bold octagonal angle turrets terminating in noble pinnacles, with enriched battlements and parapet, and smaller central pinnacles.

St. Olave Jewry, Old Jewry, was erected in 1673, and rises to a height of about 88 feet to top of obelisks. It consists of four stories, containing on the lowermost one a square-headed door, with Doric side columns, entablature, and cambered pediment; the second story is pierced by a circular-headed window, and emphasized by a pronounced moulded string course; the third story contains the clock and case, with pediment over, and side consoles; the belfry stage is pierced by circular-headed openings edged with moulded architraves, and having centre and cross mullions, and filled in with louvres.

An enriched cornice with plain parapet, and angle-piers supporting obelisks with balls on top, veiling flat lead roof, complete the tower. In the centre a tall flag-staff carries a vane surmounted by a gilded ship. The flag-staff is now utilized for the prosaic purposes of a telegraph post.

Westminster Abbey.— Western Towers.—In 1713 Wren drew up a Report upon the state of the Abbey for the Bishop of Rochester, in which he says—"The West Front is very requisite to be finished, because the two towers are not of equal height, and too low for the bells, which hang so much lower than the roof, that they are not heard so far as they should be. . . . The two western towers ought certainly to be carried to an equal height, one story above the ridge of the roof, still continuing the Gothic manner in the stonework and tracery. . . . I have prepared perfect draughts and models (drawings) such as I conceive may agree with the original scheme of the old architect, without any modern mixtures to show my own inventions."

Mr. Fergusson, in his "History of Modern Architecture," says of them, "Their proportions are perfect, though their details deviate more from the Gothic type than is the case in his other examples. If they are really his—though this is more than doubtful—this was a singular mistake for such an architect to make."

In Dean Stanley's "Memorials" of the Abbey, the western towers by Wren are mentioned as having been finished, and, considering the Abbey documents at the Dean's command, this statement would hardly have been made without due substantiation. Besides, their beauty of proportion and treatment are in such harmony with Wren's other works, and knowing as we do that he made designs for them, I think that we can hardly hesitate to accept them as Wren's own work. The carelessness of Gothic detail evinced need not astonish us, as we found in the case of St. Michael's, Cornhill, and others, that Wren was not careful to obtain the correct details, even when such could easily have been obtained, the feeling doubtless being at that time, that to make Gothic at all palatable, it was necessary to give it a semi-Classic dress. Indeed, the wonder might rather

be that these towers were not altogether Classic, for we know
that Inigo Jones attached a Corinthian portico to the west
end of old St. Paul's, and no one seemed to have thought it an
anachronism.   We must judge of these things in the light of the
times in which they took place.   Have we never heard in our
own time of Gothic porches and other additions being made to
Classic buildings ?   Nevertheless, one cannot but regret that
to the fine proportions had not been joined correct detail, so as
to have given us towers altogether worthy to guard a shrine of
St. Peter, and make a beautiful and perfect harmony in stone.

It may not be out of place here to mention that Wren also
contemplated the completion of the central tower and spire, for
in the same Report from which I have already quoted he goes
on to say, " The original intention was plainly to have had a spire,
the beginnings of which appear on the corners of the cross, but
left off before it rose so high as the ridge of the roof. . . In
my opinion the tower should be continued to at least as much in
height above the roof, as it is in breadth'; and if a spire be added
to it, it will give a proper grace to the whole fabric, and the west
end of the city, which seems to want it. · I have made a design
which will not be very expensive, but light, and still in the Gothic
form, and of a style with the rest of the structure, which I would
strictly adhere to throughout the whole intention.   To deviate
from the old form would be to run into a disagreeable mixture,
which no person of a good taste could relish.   I have varied a
little from the usual form, in giving twelve sides to the spire
instead of eight, for reasons to be discerned in the model.   The
angles of pyramids in the Gothic architecture were usually enriched
with the flower the botanists call calceolus, which is a proper form
to help workmen to ascend on the outside to amend any defects,
without raising large scaffolds.   I have done the same, as being
of so good use, as well as agreeable ornament."

However much one might have desired to see what Wren would have made of this,—feeling sure that it would have been worthy of his genius; yet considering his imperfect knowledge of Gothic, we cannot be altogether sorry that his central tower and spire was not carried out; but that it has been left for a second Wren, with a more perfect understanding of Gothic—should he arise—to complete it.

We shall now consider the Steeples, Spires, and Towers in London which have been pulled down, of which there are ten.

St. Antholin (or St. Anthony), Watling Street, was erected in 1682, and was the only stone spire, pure and simple, which Wren carried out. It measured 20 ft. 6 in. at base, and rose to a height of 154 feet to top of spire. The upper portion of the belfry stage was octagonal, with circular-headed openings filled in with louvres on the four sides, the square tower being reduced to the octagon by semi-circular turrets at the angles. A projecting cornice and triple blocking-course surmounted the tower, from which sprang an octagonal, panelled stone spire, 70 feet high. The base of this was pierced by eight square-headed openings filled in with louvres, having cornices and pediments over each. Two rows of small elliptical openings pierced the spire in the height, which was finished by a Corinthian capital surmounted by a finial and vane. The simple construction is shown on the section. It was pulled down in 1875. One cannot but deeply regret the loss of this spire, unique in its way amongst Wren's works; especially as it could very well have been allowed to remain, and indeed did remain for a short time after the Church was pulled down; but the increased price which was thereby obtainable for the site, finally outweighing all

Pl. 12.

All Hallows the Great
Thomas St.

S. Antholin
Watling St.

St. Dionis Backchurch
Fenchurch St.

S. Mildred
Poultry's

All Hallows
Bread St.

S. Benetfink
Threadneedle St.

S. Michael
Crooked Lane

S. Benet
Gracechurch
St.

S. Michael
Queenhithe

All pulled down.

less mercenary considerations, it shared the fate of the church: and " the place that once knew it, knows it no more for ever."

***

All Hallows the Great, Thames Street.—Although the church still stands, the tower was taken down some years ago to make room for the traffic. It was of stone, and appears to have risen to a height of about 86 feet, and was divided into four stories externally; the lowermost one containing a circular-headed doorway; the second and third stories, small windows, the upper one being circular; and the belfry openings having circular heads, moulded architraves, and key-stones. An enriched cornice with pierced parapet over, with angle piers, flanking a flat lead roof, surmounted the whole. The tower was simple, but, like all Wren's works, of good and pleasing proportions.

***

All Hallows, Bread Street, and St. John Evangelist, Watling Street, was erected in 1697, and stood at the corner of Bread Street and Watling Street. It was interesting as being the church in which Milton was baptized. It was but recently pulled down. The tower measured 17 ft. 6 in. at base, and rose to a height of about 86 feet, or about 104 to the top of the obelisks. It consisted of five stories, the lowermost one containing a doorway with an elliptical pediment; the second and third stories had circular windows in each; the fourth, a window with moulded architrave and carved festoon of fruit and flowers over. The belfry stage had an arcade of triple openings on each face, with masks carved on the keystones. A cornice and balustrade, having angle-piers supporting obelisks, surmounted the whole.

St. Benet, Gracechurch Street was erected in 1685, and stood at the corner of Fenchurch Street and Gracechurch Street. It measured about 20 feet at base, and rose to a total height of 149 feet.

The tower was comparatively plain up to belfry stage, where it was enriched by a cornice and pediment on each face, having beneath, belfry openings with circular heads, rising into the tympanum, the cornice being stopped at each side of same. Above this the tower rose plain until it cleared the pediments, whence sprung a lead-covered cupola, panelled, to a height of about 12 feet, which supported a lantern, having the belfry features repeated on a diminutive scale. On top a square panelled base was set, from which rose a tall panelled obelisk 26 feet high, resting on balls, and terminating with a finial and vane.

St. Benedict (or St. Benet Fink), stood on the north side of Threadneedle Street, and was erected in 1673. The tower measured 18 ft. 9 in. at base, and rose to a total height of 101 feet. The accompanying section shows the construction, in which the walls will be seen to be of unusual thickness. The whole composition, with its oval belfry openings, its lead-covered swelling cupola, and its neat lantern, although unpretentious, must have been very pleasing.

St. Christopher, Threadneedle Street, was not totally destroyed by the Great Fire, and with the Gothic tower was only repaired by Wren in 1671, and beautified in 1696. The whole was taken down in 1781 to enlarge the Bank of England.

Pl. 13.

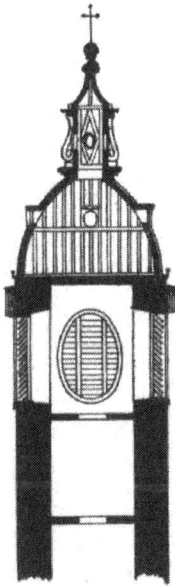

S. Benet Fink.
Threadneedle St.
pulled down

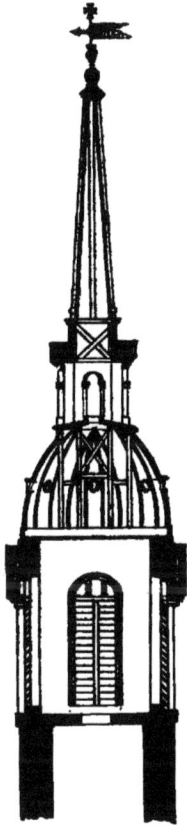

S. Benet
Gracechurch St.
pulled down.

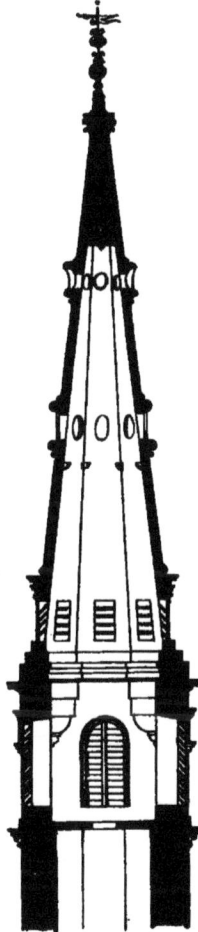

·S. Antholin·
·Watling St.·
·*pulled down*

St. Dionis Backchurch, was erected in 1684, nearly ten years after the church, and stood at the corner of Fenchurch and Lime Streets. It was so called from having originally stood behind a row of houses, and to distinguish it from another church which, previous to the Great Fire, stood in the middle of Fenchurch Street. It has only recently been pulled down, the site proving itself since a regular bone of contention. The tower was of stone, and rose to a height of about 90 feet, including turret. It was divided into four stories, the lowermost one containing the doorway; the next two stories were pierced by small windows, and the belfry stage, with circular-headed openings, having moulded architraves and square cornice over. A bold stone cornice, balustrade, and angle piers crowned the tower. Within this a small open turret rose, of simple design.

St. Michael, Crooked Lane, was erected in 1698, but as it stood directly in the line of the approaches to New London Bridge, it was pulled down in 1830. The tower did not vary in character from many others, but the lofty and prominent lead lantern was of an extremely bold and original type. It consisted of three stories, timber-framed and covered with lead, and was circular, with boldly projecting buttresses at the four angles of tower, to bring it to the square; each story was pierced with openings, and the whole was crowned with a small cupola and lofty vane and cross.

St. Michael, Queenhithe, formerly stood at the south-west angle of Little Trinity Lane and Thames Street. It was erected in 1677, and is stated to have measured 135 feet to top of spirelet. The belfry stage had square openings, with moulded architraves and cornice over. Above this a cornice and high parapet surmounted the tower, with piers supporting ornaments at angles. Over this a curious stepped truncated pyramid rose, framed in timber, and covered with lead, supporting a square lantern, with double apertures on each face, which was again surmounted by a panelled lead spirelet, terminating in a vane in the form of a ship. The composition appears to have been more curious than beautiful.

St. Mildred, Poultry, was erected in 1676, and stood on the north side of the Poultry. The tower rose to a height of about 75 feet, and was of stone, and more ornate than many of them· It was divided into three stories, the ground story containing a doorway, with projecting hood supported on cantilevers; the second story had a circular headed window, with pilasters, consoles, entablature, and pediment over; the belfry stage had square-headed openings with moulded architraves, each opening being encased in a large sunk panel. A bold cornice and unpierced parapet finished the tower. From the flat roof rose a small square turret, with wide openings on each face, and surmounted by a small cupola supporting a vane.

It now remains to consider the Towers and Steeples of Wren's designing—outside of London.

These are few, and not strikingly important, so that any who desire to study Wren's towers, &c., will find nearly all within a radius of half a mile from St. Paul's Cathedral.

Outside, we shall find one at Warwick and one at Oxford, viz.: St. Mary, Warwick, and the Entrance Gateway Tower of Christ Church College, Oxford. Mr. Fergusson is of opinion that the twin towers and lanterns of All Souls College, Oxford, are by Wren; but his pupil, Hawksmoor, is almost universally credited with them, and I cannot find evidence sufficient to outweigh this. Mr. Fergusson bases his opinion on the fact that they are too good for any but Wren; but it is to be remembered that Hawksmoor was his most gifted pupil, and has done other good work elsewhere.

The parish church of Isleworth-on-Thames is also attributed to Wren, and correctly enough so far, for we know that he furnished designs in 1701 for a new church, and that in 1705 his design was partially carried out. The old Gothic tower, however, remained, overgrown with ivy.

St. Mary, Warwick.—The church was partly burned in a destructive fire in 1694, and the destroyed portions, together with the tower, were rebuilt in 1704, when the rest of the church was generally repaired. The towers measures 117 feet high to the top of the battlements, and 25 feet more to the top of the pinnacles; it cost £1,600. A Latin inscription cut in three faces of the tower tells how it was destroyed and rebuilt in the " glorious reign of Queen Anne." It consists of three main stories, each of these being subdivided; the ground story is arched and vaulted, forming an open arcade; columns up the face of the tower form angle piers, which are relieved by niches. A double tier of belfry openings occupy the upper stage, and the cornice is crowned by an ornate and pierced double parapet, with angle and centre crocketted pinnacles. The beauties and defects of Wren's Gothic designs are conspicuous here,—the former, in the fine proportion, dignity, and balance of the different parts; the latter, in the admixture of the two styles, and the incongruity of the detail.

44

Entrance Tower, Christ Church College, Oxford.—Cardinal
Wolsey had left this tower unfinished. In 1681 Wren furnished
a design for its completion, which in the following year was
carried out. To be in keeping with the rest, Wren was
compelled to adopt Gothic, and although it is not free'from the
faults of all his Gothic conceptions, yet it is extremely graceful
in shape and contour, and almost noble; and in the disposition
of its parts, and the refinement of its features, is not unworthy
to crown Wolsey's work.

I have not mentioned the Monument of London amongst
Wren's Steeples and Towers, as it can hardly be classed in that
category; but in the beauty of its shape and appropriateness
of expression it is unsurpassed by any other similar column,
ancient or modern.

I may also mention that the upper portion of Chichester Spire
was rebuilt under Wren's direction, and an ingenious pendulum
stage was designed by him to counteract the effect of the wind.

Having thus gone over in detail all the Steeples and Towers
designed by Sir Christopher Wren, as far as I have been able
to discover, there can be but one feeling in regard to them,—
that such legacies should be reverently received, cherished,
and preserved.

It would be beyond the scope of this work to enter into
a consideration of the ecclesiastical view of the subject,—
whether it is expedient to pull down some of these churches
and towers from which the population has receded, and, with
the large sums obtainable for the sites, build and endow other
churches in new neighbourhoods to which the population
has migrated; but I may venture to say, that even from this

point of view there is a beautiful fitness in Houses of Prayer intermingling with the Halls of Commerce—quiet resting-places, where in intervals of toil the harassed man of business could turn aside to get the wrinkles smoothed from his spirit, and the fever of "the haste to be rich" allayed: and I cannot but think that faithful clergymen would find work enough to do, even in the City parishes. For the outlying and suburban neighbourhoods, I believe the Church has never appealed sufficiently to the Christian liberality of all its members, and that if proper steps were taken, and the right spirit abroad in the Church, there would be no lack of means wherewith to plant and carry on these new churches.

Looked at from an artistic point of view, there can be no shadow of a doubt in all sensible minds as to the paramount desirability of preserving these Memorials of Wren. Should, however, their enemies so far prevail as to pull down more of the churches, I would most earnestly plead that the towers be spared. It may be said—"What is the use of the tower, when the church is gone?—it is an anachronism!" And though this may be true to a certain extent, yet they would serve to show where the church once stood, and preserve landmarks which are, alas! but too swiftly being effaced. In almost all cases, from their construction, they could stand independently of the church, and the space they cover is insignificant. Were it a question of building these now, there might be reasonable excuse for hesitation, but when they *are* built, and rise into the air with a halo of two centuries around them, to deliberately raze them to the ground, is surely the grossest Vandalism.

What is it which gives London its unique appearance? It is its numerous towers and spires clustering around St. Paul's, like a people around their prince. There is hardly a finer sight than to look from above the Dome of St. Paul's, or from the top of the Monument, over the sea of houses stretching on every side, until they vanish into the smoke and mist, — pierced and punctuated by the steeples and towers, of varied design and beauty. Imagine the same scene, robbed of these, and nothing but tile and slate roofs, varied by the quintessent ugliness of chimney-pots and cowls, stretching all around into weary distance! London, instead of being the worthy capital of the British Empire, would simply become an ugly piece of mechanism for money-making.

Already ten of Wren's churches have disappeared under the " Union of Benefices Act" of 1860, and from other causes ; and under a scheme drawn up by the Fellows of Zion College in 1876, thirty-one more City churches were marked for destruction! This, however, was too much even for the apathy of the British public, and steps were taken to resist such a scheme, which were so far successful that the matter has been allowed to drop for the present ; but it may be resuscitated at any time, and it is imperatively necessary, therefore, that a greater public interest be awakened in the Churches, that we be not implicated in deeds for which posterity will not hold us blameless.

The Church and Churchyard Protection Society has done good work, and has saved at least one, recently; but more requires to be done. And for these Churches and Towers which have already been destroyed, I would venture to suggest that on the site of them, in all cases, there should be placed a permanent record, and a reliable representation of the tower and church as they stood, either in the form of a Brass, or incised work on a marble tablet. Something of this kind has been done for St. Antholin's in fresco work; but a more permanent material, and a more spirited execution, seems desirable.

These creations of Wren's genius ought to be dear to every Englishman, and especially to every Londoner; they are monu-

ments of an intensely interesting chapter of history; they are
memorials of the faith, the fervour, and the piety of the nation
at a period of harassing troubles and anxieties; they are the very
soul of a man of whom England should ever be proud—an
architect sprung from and nourished by herself, and worthy to
be placed in the first rank of men of genius of all time.

Printed by W. KNOTT, 26, Brooke Street, Holborn, E.C.

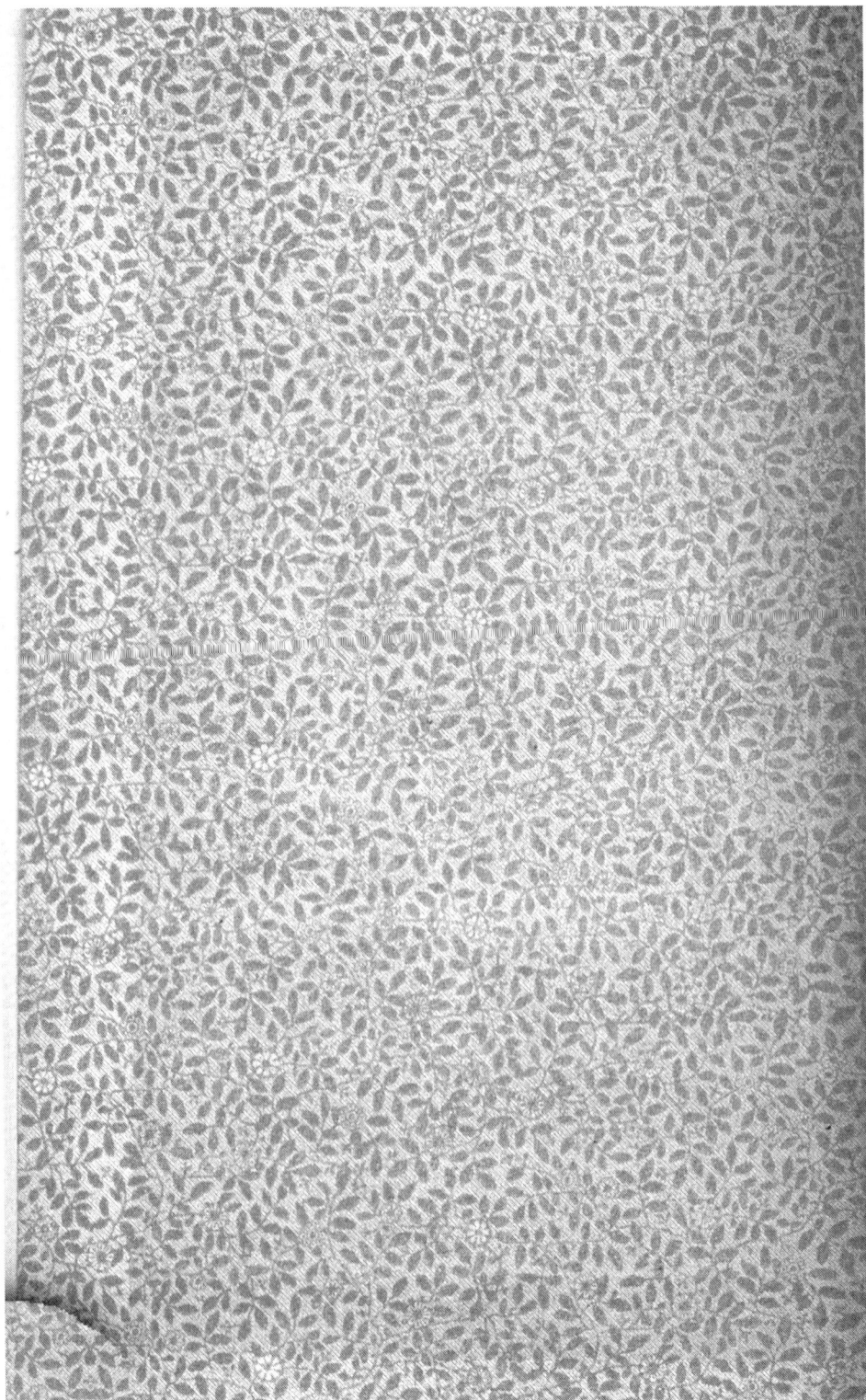

Lightning Source UK Ltd.
Milton Keynes UK
UKHW022246110121
376855UK00008B/1723

9 781377 254906